Light on Old Sayings

by
JOHN LASTINGHAM

illustrated by
KEN ROBINSON

MOWBRAY
LONDON & OXFORD

© A. R. Mowbray & Co. Ltd 1986
Illustrations © Ken Robinson

ISBN 0 264 67105 8

This edition first published 1986 by
A. R. Mowbray & Co. Ltd,
Saint Thomas House, Becket Street,
Oxford, OX1 1SJ

The text and illustrations in this book were first
reproduced in *The Sign* magazine over a period of several
years.

Printed in Great Britain by Cox and Wyman Ltd,
Reading

Cover design, typesetting and layout by Comersgate Art
Studios, Oxford.

British Library Cataloguing in Publication Data

Lastingham, John
  Light on old sayings.—(Mowbray leisure
  series)
  1. Proverbs, English—Caricatures and
  cartoons
  I. Title II. Robinson, Ken
  398′.9′ 210207 NC1763.P77/

ISBN 0-264-67105-8

KenRobinson -

To get out of bed the wrong side in the morning

To start the day in a grumpy mood. It was an ancient and strong superstition that it was unlucky to set the left foot on the floor on first getting out of bed in the morning. The same superstition applied to putting on the left shoe first.

1

Born with a silver spoon in the mouth

To be born to good fortune or to wealth. The phrase originates with the custom of godfathers or godmothers presenting a silver spoon to a child. The lucky child does not have to wait for the gift because it inherits wealth and fortune at birth.

- KenRobinson -

To make oneself at home

To act familiarly in someone else's house, not to act on ceremony, or to be on best behaviour. Just as in our own homes and familiar surroundings we act in a relaxed manner, so we can in other people's homes sometimes do the same. The phrase can also mean being at ease in any particular situation.

-KEN ROBINSON-

To gird up the loins

To prepare for a hard piece of work, or any arduous enterprise. Eastern peoples, as in Bible times, commonly wore flowing garments. When they wished to be active they tucked them up out of the way. The Bible often uses the phrase, as in 'Gird up your loins like a man' (Job 38.3).

4

To get the wind up

To become frightened and nervous. In the early days of flying, when pilots had to stretch their legs out in mid air to reach the rudder bar in order to control the aircraft, any sudden fall of the plane in an air pocket would cause the wind to rush up and give him a fright.

To be stiff necked

To be obstinate, difficult, to control or reach, to be self-willed. This is a very old phrase that occurs at least twice in the Bible; 'Speak not with a stiff neck' is in Psalm 75.5. 'They obey not, but made their necks stiff' is in Isaiah 48.4. The metaphor comes from the idea of a wilful horse which will not be controlled by the reins, but keeps its neck stiff and unresponsive.

To touch someone on the raw

To say something particularly hurtful, making the hearer wince or start. When a horse was curried, or had his skin brushed, the groom might accidentally touch him on a raw place, so that the horse feeling a sudden pain, might start away.

To win by a walkover

To have a very easy victory. The background to this
phrase comes from athletics. If a competitor in a
running race draws so far ahead of the others in it
that he is able to reach the final tape by slowing
down to a walking pace but still winning he is said
to have 'a walkover'.

To set your cap at someone

To try to attract someone, traditionally used of the efforts of a girl to capture the attentions of a man. The phrase began in the days when ladies habitually wore caps indoors. They would naturally put on the most becoming to attract the attention and admiration of a possible suitor.

To cut a caper

To act in an unusual manner. Usually with the object of attracting notice. The origin of this lies in the Italian word cappra, meaning a she goat, an allusion to the erratic way in which goats will, for no apparent reason, leap about, playing 'the giddy goat'.

To wear the heart on the sleeve

To expose secret intentions to general notice. It was once the custom for a man to tie his lady's favour, such as a ribbon or rosette, on his sleeve. Thus exposing his affections. Iago in Shakespeare's *Othello* uses the phrase when he says: But I will wear my heart upon my sleeve.

- KenRobinson

To talk hot air

To speak in a bombastic way and at the same time a nonsensical manner. The origin of the phrase lies in the use of hot air to inflate a balloon. When introduced into the bag, the hot air expands the envelope until the whole thing rises up and floats away.

To stretch a point

To relax in an argument. The 'point' in question was
the tagged laced-end of the strings used to lace up
those ladies striving for the 'hour-glass' figure of
their day. After dining well, and with dancing to
follow, it was often vital to loosen and 'stretch a
point'.

To leave no stone unturned

To spare no trouble, time or expense in trying to accomplish an aim. After the defeat of a Persian general, Mardomius, at Plataea in 477BC, it was reported that he had left great treasures in his tent. But these could not be found by his conquerors. So the Oracle of Delphi was consulted and said that they should 'leave no stone unturned'. So when this command was obeyed, the treasures were discovered.

To make bricks without straw

To attempt to do something without the proper and necessary materials. The phrase comes from the Book of Exodus 5.5-7. 'And Pharaoh said: "Behold, the people of the land are many and you make them rest from their burdens!" The same day Pharaoh commanded the taskmaster to the people and their foremen, "You shall no longer give the people straw to make bricks, as heretofore. Let them go and gather straw for themselves".'

To be not up to the mark

To fall below the standard required. This phrase comes from the practice of having gold and silver articles marked by the assay office to indicate that they satisfy an agreed standard of quality. Any object falling short of this standard is said to be 'not up to the mark'.

To have the odour of sanctity

To give an impression of holiness, or of exceptionally high moral tone. In the Middle Ages it was believed that a delightful odour was given off by the bodies of saintly persons after their death. Many legends exist of a sweet smell arising from the tomb of a saintly person when it was opened, as, for example, in the case of St Etheldreda of Ely, when she was disinterred to be given a grander burial.

To win one's spurs

To prove one's self. In olden times when a man was knighted, he was presented with a pair of gilt spurs as a mark of the honour which he had received.

To be in someone's good books

To be held in favour by another person. The word
'book' was at one time used to mean a single sheet,
or even a list was called a book. Therefore to be in
someone's good books, meant to be on his list of
friends. The writer Addison uses the expression
when he says: 'I was so much in his books, that at
his decease he left me his lamp.'

To be led by the nose

To be taken in a particular direction, possibly in a false one, through inability to resist. This phrase comes from the ancient practice of leading some animals, such as bulls, camels, and captive bears, through rings inserted in their nostrils. The point made is that a person who is 'led by the nose' has very little power of resistance and just goes where he is led.

To be a stormy petrel

*To be a trouble maker, a person whose arrival on a
scene usually means bother.* Small seabirds called
Petrels were originally so named, according to
tradition, from the Italian Petrello, meaning little
Peter. During stormy weather these birds seem to
fly along patting the water with each foot alternately
as though walking on it, reminiscent of Saint Peter
who walked on the Sea of Galilee. Their association
with stormy weather led to the use of the name to
betoken stormy kind of people.

21

To go haywire

To run riot, to behave in an uncontrolled manner.
This is an American phrase which arose from the
difficulty of handling the coils of wire used for
binding bundles of hay. If such a coil was fastened
unskilfully it sprang out in great loops and quickly
became unmanageable.

To eat humble pie

To be abject before some person, or continually in a position of seeming inferiority. The correct term is UMBLE pie, and UMBLE pie is still made in some remote parts of England. Umble pie contains the odds and ends of the edible inward parts of an animal. It was popular among the poor, and was served by the master of the house to the servants and menials on his estate.

To have an axe to grind

To have some personal interest in a matter. The
phrase comes from the story of a man who, wishing
to grind his axe, had no time to turn the grindstone.
He therefore asked a boy to show him how the
machine worked, and kept praising him until the
axe was ground.

To play second fiddle

To take a subordinate or secondary part. First violin, or first fiddle, in any orchestra, is the Leader. So second fiddle, or second violin, necessarily ranks one step down.

To be hard up

To be short of money. This was originally a nautical phrase. When a ship was caught in severe weather the order would be given 'hard up the helm'. Then the tiller was put up as far as possible to windward so as to turn the ship's head away from the wind. So, when someone is 'hard up' he has to weather the storm as best he may.

To make the hair stand on end

To take fright. It has long been thought that fright can actually make the hair rise. There is a striking mention of this in the Book of Job (4.15), when Eliphaz says 'His spirit glided past my face; the hair of my flesh stood up.'

To nail a lie to the counter

To make certain that truth in a confused situation is clearly visible to all. This saying deals with the means used to denounce a person offering a counterfeit coin, in a day when this deception was much more common than now. When a counterfeit coin was found among a shopkeeper's takings, it was at once nailed to the counter in a prominent position.

Strike while the iron is hot

To catch the right moment. A blacksmith making a horse shoe has to strike the metal with his hammer when it is red hot and exactly the right temperature, otherwise it cannot be moulded into the correct shape. So this phrase comes straight out of the blacksmith's forge.

To have no shot in one's locker

To be hard up, or to have no further resources. The phrase comes from the days of the old men of war, when ammunition was kept in lockers. When this ammunition was used up the ship could no longer be in action. It was therefore unable to make a positive response to a challenge, or indeed to carry out any of the functions for which it was designed.

To cut and run

*To get out of a situation as quickly as possible,
without bothering about what might be left behind.*
This is a phrase which comes from the days of sail,
when, if a ship was overtaken by a sudden and
unexpected crisis, the only thing to do was to cut
the cable, if necessary leaving the rest of it,
including the anchor, behind, and running before
the wind.

KenRobinson

To put your thinking cap on

To give careful thought to a matter before coming to a final decision. There was a time when judges in court always put on a cap before passing any sentence. Eventually it was done only for passing the death sentence in the days of capital punishment. Now, of course, it is not done at all; but the phrase remains.

To give a wide berth

To take care to avoid a source of danger. When a ship was anchored by the bows she needed plenty of room to swing at anchor, as tide or wind varied. In other words, she needed a wide berth and it was a good idea to keep a distance from her.

To play to the gallery

To work for popularity. When an actor wished to
draw the applause of people high up in the gallery
of a theatre, he would often have to exaggerate the
words he was speaking, and so sacrifice the quality
and sense of his lines in order to gain popular
acclaim.

KEN ROBINSON

To upstage someone

To put another person down by assuming airs of consequence and superiority. This comes from the language of the theatre. Most stages slope slightly from the footlights up towards the rear. So an actor 'upstage' that is, towards the rear, is in a position to speak towards other players near the front.

To have itching ears

To enjoy hearing news, scandal, or gossip. The phrase originates in a passage from 2 Timothy 4.3, 'People will not listen to sound doctrine, but will follow their own desires and will collect for themselves more and more teachers who will tell them what they are itching to hear.' It was once supposed that the itching of various parts of the body indicated that they would shortly be involved in some happening, or would wish to be, like having an itching palm when money was wanted.

To go on a wild goose chase

To embark on a senseless undertaking. Because a wild
goose was notoriously difficult, if not impossible to
catch, the idea of chasing after it came to represent a
senseless undertaking without a hope of success.
And since a wild goose was not worth having,
anyway, even if it ever was caught, to go on a wild
goose chase also showed a lack of common sense.

To act like a vandal

Wantonly to destroy property, especially objects of value. To act in a savage manner. The vandals were a Teutonic race who in the fifty century AD ravaged Gaul, the modern France, and eventually captured Rome. They despoiled the eternal city of its treasures of art without any other apparent reason than their own ignorance and savagery.

To kick over the traces

To act independently; to go off on a course of one's own suddenly. In the days of horse transport it was sometimes difficult to get the animal to run in harness with other horses. One who refused would literally 'kick over the traces', that is, part of the harness gear, and run away on his own.

To speak Bunkum

To talk nonsense. A representative at Washington regularly made long and flowery speeches with the purpose of ingratiating himself into the favour of his constituents at Buncombe. On being challenged he admitted he was not speaking to the House but as he said 'I was speaking to Buncombe' which has become our present day BUNKUM.

To put a spoke in his wheel

To cause a sudden stop to a plan or enterprise. A
spoke in the wheel was the common and crude form
of braking in ancient days. Three holes were drilled
into the wooden rim of a wheel. This gave the driver
three chances of putting a spoke in, which simply
meant inserting a loose piece of wood into any one
of the holes so that it would jam against the
underside of the cart and, being jammed, would
drag along the ground, and slow the cart.

KEN ROBINSON

To come up to scratch

To be shown capable of a task. In the old days of
bare-fisted prize-fighting, before there was any
proper ring, a line used to be scratched on the
ground in the middle of the combat area. When the
fighters were called out, each had to toe the line or
'come up to the scratch'. The fight could then start.

To be on the ropes

To be up against it. To be in an exceptionally difficult position. This comes from the terminology of the boxing ring, where the ropes surrounding it mark the edges of the area. A boxer fought back against the ropes, and probably being hammered by his opponent, literally is 'on the ropes' and is in an awkward spot.

The real McCoy

Something genuine and right up to standard. 'Kid McCoy' was an early-day American prizefighter of exceptional courage and great skill. After his passing from the boxing scene, there were ambitious young men who adopted his name, but none of them ever found the skill or courage of 'the real McCoy', hence the term.

To throw up the sponge

To give in, to surrender. In the old days of prize fights, a second would toss a sponge into the air as a sign that his man was beaten.

To ear-mark

To set something aside for a particular purpose. This saying comes from the custom of putting owners' marks on the ears of cattle and sheep. Animals marked in this way can often be seen in the fields. From this practice has come the use of the phrase to indicate the designation of some particular purpose for a grant or payment. It is still very much in current use, as when, for example, a treasurer can say that he has 'ear-marked' a certain amount of money for this or that purpose.

On the stocks

To have some job in hand and awaiting completion.
The term comes from ship-building, where the
stocks are the frame in which a ship is placed while
under construction. So long as it is there, it is said
to be 'on the stocks', in other words, in the course of
construction.

Cut and dried

Sometimes used of an argument, or point of view, the phrase means that it is completely prepared. The origin of the phrase lies in the custom of preparing timber for use. After a tree is felled, the timber needs to be cut up into lengths, and dried. Dean Swift, in one of his verses, showed the use of the phrase when he wrote:

Sets of phrases, cut and dry, ever more thy tongue survive.

To have too many irons in the fire

To have so many concerns on hand at the same time that they can't properly be dealt with. This comes from the blacksmith's forge where, if the smith had too many irons heating at the same time, he couldn't deal with them before some had cooled off.

He is not fit to hold a candle to him

To be unworthy of comparison. Before artificial
lighting such as electricity was available, lighting
boys (as they were called) were hired in the theatre
to hold a candle near to an actor, particularly near
enough to his face to show the particular emotions
he was registering. This was a duty requiring great
skill and understanding.

KEN ROBINSON

The devil take the hind most

A warning that there are dangers in being last. This phrase really comes from belief in magic in olden times. At a school on Toledo, in Spain, it was said that when the students had progressed up to a certain point in their studies, they were compelled to run through an underground hall as a test. The last man was always chased by the devil and, when captured, became his imp.

Tempering the wind to the shorn lamb

To make allowances for physical or other weakness.
The phrase was used by Laurence Stern in his book
The Sentimental Journey. It was originally 'God
tempers the wind to the shorn lamb'. The phrase
was not original, however, and Stern rather spoilt
the effect by substituting 'lamb' for 'sheep', because
lambs are in fact never shorn.

To be not worth one's salt

To be undeserving of wages or other reward, or to be inadequate for some particular task and therefore not deserving of paying for it. This phrase comes from the practice in ancient times of paying what were called 'salt rations' to Roman soldiers as part of their wages. The Latin word *salarium* from which comes our 'salary' means salt. When money payments began to be used instead of this salt issue the same name continued to be used for wages.

Letting the cat out of the bag

To disclose some hidden facts. It used to be an old country trick to substitute a cat for a sucking pig, put it in a sack and take it to market for sale. If anyone bought without opening the sack, then they were duly taken in. But if they opened it then the cat really was out of the bag and the deception made known.

KEN ROBINSON

Blowing your own trumpet

Singing your own praises. The origin of this goes
back to the time of heralds, who used to announce
with a great flourish of trumpets the knights who
entered the lists to joust with each other. Or
sometimes a herald would blow a trumpet to call
attention to an important messenger or emissary.

What the trumpeter never did, was to blow his
instrument in order to announce himself. So to
blow one's own trumpet is to show off in a big way.

A pretty kettle of fish

An awkward state of affairs, a mess. An old Border name for a picnic by the riverside in which newly caught salmon were the chief dish was a kettle of fish. But the preparation was difficult and often went wrong. When this happened the result was 'a pretty kettle of fish'.

Upsetting the apple cart

To overthrow an arrangement or plan. When a
farmer had a load of apples, which he was taking to
market, and by accident the cart was overturned,
his hopes of a profitable sale were lost, because the
fruit would be damaged as well as scattered. The
phrase comes from the late eighteenth century and
is first recorded as in use in 1796.

Not worth a rap

Something worth nothing at all. The origin of this
lies in the fact that in eighteenth century Ireland a
coin in circulation was a base halfpenny worth
about half a farthing and called a rap.
Consequently, it was without value.

Pin money

Cash set by as a result of some secondary employment.
Nowadays, when wives as well as daughters, often
go out to work and earn their own money, this
question of an allowance rarely arises. But, long
ago, before the time of mass production, when pins
were very expensive, it was helpful for a woman to
have a special allowance to buy them.

A dog in a manger

*An obstructive person concerned to obstruct the
enjoyment of others for no good reason.* The origin of
the phrase is the ancient fable of a dog which got
into the habit of lying in a manger. Yet, although as
a dog he could not eat the hay, at the same time he
would growl when the ox, which could, came near,
so denying the other what he could not use himself.

A bird of ill-omen

A man or woman who is looked upon as unlucky, as a person in the habit of bringing ill-news. This phrase comes from Roman times when there was a religious official who professed to tell future events.

Dead as a door nail

To be completely finished and done with. The door
nail is the knob upon which the door knocker
strikes. As it is often knocked on the head it can be
assumed to have no life left in it. The phrase is very
old. Shakespeare uses it in *Henry IV Part Two*, act 4
scene 10. 'Come thou and thy five men, and if I do
not leave you all as dead as a door nail, I pray God I
may never leave Grass moor.'

To bite the dust

To be conquered, or over-thrown. This is a dramatic
way of saying that someone has been thrown to the
ground or generally overpowered. It originates
from the western stories of Buffalo Bill who was
said to have slain enormous numbers of red indians
in the early days of the Wild West. Popular
accounts of his supposed exploits would say that
'Another redskin bit the dust'.

To steal a march

To take advantage by a stratagem. The phrase comes
from times when armies moved on foot, so that
their time of arrival before a battle could be roughly
foretold. Buf if they 'stole a march', probably by
moving at night, they could spring a surprise on the
enemy.

Keeping your powder dry

To be prepared for action at all times. The story comes from one told of Oliver Cromwell who during a campaign in Ireland addressed his troops just before they were going to cross a river to make an attack. He said, 'Put your trust in God; but be sure to keep your powder dry.'

Blood is thicker than water

Family relationships are likely to be more lasting than those without such a link. This very old proverb springs from the fact that while water soon evaporates, leaving no trace, blood leaves a stain. The idea is that the concern we might have for someone with a family link is likely to be more lasting than that which we might have for a stranger.

A bigwig

An important person. In the seventeenth and eighteenth centuries large wigs, covering the head and shoulders, were worn by the aristocracy. They still are worn by such people as the Lord Chancellor, Judges, and Barristers. Bishops used to wear them until 1880. So it was a case of the bigger the wig the greater the importance.

The weakest go to the wall

Pews were not available in any great numbers in churches until the late sixteenth century. Such pews as were available were the preserve of the influential and the rich.

However, Christian concern made it necessary for some seating to be provided for the very old, and disabled. Wooden benches were provided around the walls of the church, for the use of the weak and aged.

Robbing Peter to pay Paul

To take away from one person in order to give to another. In 1550 the Abbey Church of St Peter, Westminster, was created a cathedral. Ten years later, when it was rejoined to the Diocese of London, many of its estates were appropriated to the repairs of St Paul's Cathedral. So the abbey lost what St Paul's gained.

A lick and a promise

To do a piece of work in a hasty and superficial way.
A cat who can often be seen to begin washing its
face with one quick lick of its tongue on its paw, and
then moving the paw briefly over the face.
Obviously, there is promise of more cleaning to
come later. Meanwhile a start has been made; but
nothing else – certainly not a good wash!

Before you can say Jack Robinson

An event which takes place very quickly. The saying
originated with a man really called Jack Robinson
who used to pay such quick visits to his neighbours
that he was gone before the servant could announce
his name.

On the nose

To be on cue. The phrase comes from the early days
of sound broadcasting when the producer,
signalling to the performers in the studio, would
put his finger on his nose when the programme was
running exactly on time.

Ken Robinson.

To be out of gear

To be not in working order, to be out of sorts. If a car
is not in gear its engine cannot move it forward, so
that it is, in effect, not in working order. In the
same way, if a person's mood is wrong, or if they
happen to be in ill health, then similarly they cannot
cope with life.

Caught napping

To be surprised when taking time off. Cats are
particularly prone to this – hence the phrase
'cat-nap'. But several other animals have this habit,
and were often caught while doing so; in other
words, 'caught napping'.

To get the sack

To lose one's job, to be dismissed. Mechanics and other tradesmen used to carry the tools of their trade in a bag or sack. So when they were discharged they were 'given the sack' and sent on their way to find a job somewhere else.

Hobson's choice

To have no alternative but to choose what is placed before one. Thomas Hobson in the sixteenth century was a carrier and innkeeper at Cambridge. Everyone who came to hire a horse had by his rule to take the one nearest to the stable door. The rule was that he could either take this horse or no horse. Therefore he had 'Hobson's choice'.

To go the whole hog

To do something completely and thoroughly without reservation. An old slang phrase for a shilling was a 'hog'. Therefore to go the whole hog was to spend the whole shilling at one go, and to spare nothing.

KEN ROBINSON

To carry on to the bitter end

To hang on, or to persevere until the last possible moment or time. This phrase has nothing to do with the word 'bitter'; but is a sea term meaning the end of a rope, or that part of a cable which, on a sailing vessel, was 'abaft the bitts'. Cables were fastened to bitts, wooden posts fixed in pairs on the deck. When a rope was paid out until no more of it remained, the end of these bitts was 'the bitter end', the end of the rope after which there was nothing left.